KAT

— PAINTINGS 1972 – 1996 —

— PAINTINGS 1972 – 1996 —

JACK ABSALOM

Jack Absalom points out Aboriginal rock carvings and paintings in the Red Gorge in the Bungle Bungle Ranges, Western Australia, during the filming of Jewels in the Kimberley.

LIST OF PAINTINGS

The Artist

I was born in Port Augusta, South Australia, on 11 November 1927 to an Australian father and Irish mother. My mother was born in Waterford, Ireland, but went to live in Liverpool when she was very young. Later she moved to London. My father, who had been a merchant-seaman for seven years, met my mother in London, where they were married. Mum travelled alone to Australia in 1925. My father had preceded her aboard his ship. He later left the merchant navy, and my parents settled in Port Augusta. This is where I was born, and so were my brother Reg and sister Shirley.

The world was just starting to enter the Great Depression, and from this time on things got harder until there was hardly any work for anyone. We had to shift from Port Augusta to a little place called 298. It was called this because it was 298 miles (480 kilometres) from Port Augusta, where my father got a job as a fettler on the Trans-continental Railways. After three months we were transferred to Wynbring, even further along the line. Here we had a house, and I started correspondence schooling. It was taught by the daughter of one of the other two families at the camp. Fifty years ago correspondence school was pretty rough. We used to get a lesson once a month and it would take about two hours to finish the work. Then we returned it to be corrected and had to wait another month until the next lesson came.

Because my formal schooling was so scant I had plenty of time to learn from the people I came into contact with, within the camp. I vividly remember playing with the children of Aboriginal families who moved about in groups of fifty to a hundred. They sometimes stopped at the railway camps for a few days, and often for weeks at a time. The Aboriginal men showed me the best places to set rabbit traps, but the thing I remember most about them was that they treated me like an adult. I remember collecting the cigarette butts that passengers threw out of train windows. I used to split them open and trade the tobacco with the Aborigines for small artefacts. I also sold bunches of Sturt's Desert peas to passengers and train guards. This gave me the first money I ever earned.

In 1935, my father severely injured his back while lifting a section of steel railway line and spent the next three years in hospital. The future for us without my father did not look good. At eight years of age I became the breadwinner. I trapped rabbits and sold them for threepence each. I potted and grew Sturt's Desert peas and sold them for sixpence (five cents). The railway guards and firemen soon heard of our predicament. They became helpful couriers, carrying my products to other railway camps as far as Kalgoorlie and

Perth. I reared and sold Naretha parrots and trapped dingoes and claimed the bounty. During that first year I earned twice my father's railway income.

My father finally returned home. The strapping man he had been was now doubled over, his fingertips almost touching the ground. He never totally recovered from his accident and was eventually superannuated from the railways. We returned to Port Augusta when I was about thirteen.

I had a couple of little jobs and finally got an apprenticeship on the Commonwealth Railways as an engineering smith. Throughout my apprenticeship, all my holidays were spent in the Andamooka opal fields with my uncle Andy and his wife Joyce. I would make picks and repair worn-out tools for the miners, and would make more money in those few weeks than my annual salary as an apprentice. But my father wouldn't hear of me giving up my apprenticeship. Having had such a terrible time during the Depression, he was determined that I would never be in the same position. The security that completing my apprenticeship would give me was everything to him.

In 1949 I had finished my apprenticeship and decided to head east. I stopped over in Broken Hill to visit the family of a chap I used to play football with in Port Augusta. I liked the look and feel of Broken Hill, and stayed on. This is where I met and married my wife Mary. I worked for eighteen months on the mine, constructing the above-ground steel works. In 1951, the year of my marriage, I joined the Silverton Tramway Company, and worked as their engineering blacksmith for three years. Then I started to get the urge to go out on my own — I knew that I was never going to get anywhere working for someone else. Over the years we had four businesses that started off in a small way and grew. In this period, Mary and I had started a family — we had four children.

In 1959 I thought I could make a living at kangaroo-shooting. I started out on my own in a Kombi Van, and ended up employing sixty-seven men. We had by now added an extra child to our family. For the first eighteen months I worked from Broken Hill but it soon became impossible for me to travel an additional 200 miles (320 kilometres) a night to and from Broken Hill, as well as the distance I travelled when shooting. Eventually, I was given the right to shoot on Mulyangarie Station, 100 miles (160 kilometres) from Broken Hill, and I set up a permanent camp. This ended up being the perfect place for Mary and the kids to come for school holidays.

In 1972, the Australian government literally put me out of business overnight. Bowing to pressure from local and international animal conservationists, it banned the export of kangaroo products, and the industry collapsed. I think my life was destined for a new path.

One day, one of the local bank managers asked me to guide him and a fellow artist through the Flinders Ranges on a ten-day painting trip. It was a wonderful experience. Between preparing meals and cleaning up the camp I watched them paint. Eventually I couldn't help myself any longer and I asked them if they had a spare board. They obliged, and I did three paintings straight off — I was already bitten by the bug. By the time I got back to Broken Hill I had decided to give painting a go. My family was amazed. I started off painting all day and night in a little room in the house. I loved it. I hung my paintings just about anywhere that I could find the space.

I made up my mind to paint for five years and if I could make enough money to feed my family I would not be disappointed. At first I almost gave my paintings away, because I realised that the more I had on walls the better, and if I kept my prices low people could afford to buy a couple. Things took off faster than I had imagined. Within twelve months we had so many people wanting to see my paintings that I had to have an art gallery built on the side of the house. They were selling faster than I could paint them. I put the prices up to try to slow down the sales. It was just the beginning. From the day I started painting my life took a complete turnabout. I began a lifestyle that was completely foreign to me. I was to meet and socialise with people who would change my life.

A couple of very important things happened at this time. Firstly, my gallery was put on the tourist route. This meant that we had to open every day, which is still the case, and today we have more than 60 000 visitors a year. And secondly, in 1973, I was invited by Eric Minchin to exhibit my paintings in a group exhibition in Sydney. After the success of this exhibition the 'Brushmen of the Bush' were born: Pro Hart, Hugh Schultz, John Pickup, Eric Minchin and myself. Within a couple of years we were having exhibitions in Los Angeles, New York, London and Rome. We have had duchesses, princes, governor generals and prime ministers open our exhibitions. What a special event it was to have the Duchess of Kent open our London exhibition, something none of us will ever forget. The following year the Prince of Wales opened our exhibition in Canberra. Over the years the Brushmen of the Bush have donated more than a million dollars to charities and worthy causes in Australia and overseas. Once we had been overseas we began getting international exposure.

The Australian Broadcasting Corporation contacted me at this time to make a series of television programs about Australia. I realised that everybody who watched these programs would also see my paintings, and that this would be invaluable publicity. After these programs went to air I was invited to speak at the National Press Club in Canberra.

I did another series of programs with the ABC and then made four survival programs for commercial television, showing how to handle outback hazards and how to prepare to travel safely in the outback. Altogether I have made ten one-hour and twelve half-hour television programs on various subjects concerning Australia and the outback. Between art exhibitions, painting trips and filming I wrote and published my first book Safe Outback Travel. *My first ABC program was based on this book. Since then I have written three more books, including* Outback Cooking in the Camp Oven, *and have updated* Safe Outback Travel *and had another book published, based on my ABC programs. I have more recently been a contributor to* The Great Outdoors *television programs, taking viewers to many places in Australia that I find interesting. I have also made two more one-hour programs called* Road to Adventure *— one showing how I handle caravanning, and the other one using four-wheel drive vehicles.*

Most of the paintings in this book are recent, except for a couple of favourites from my early painting years. I look back on my painting career and it's hard to believe that it all happened. Probably the highlight was in 1988, when I received the Australian Achiever of the Year award for my contribution to art. You can never be too sure in life which way the ball will bounce and what situations you will find yourself in. All this has come from doing something I love. It's unbelievable.

I hope you'll enjoy looking at the results of more than twenty years of trying.

Best wishes
Jack Absalom

The photographs that appear in this introduction were taken on location during the filming or *Rainbow's End, Jewels of the Kimberley* and *Treasures of the Pilbara*. In order of sequence, they show:

1   The type of barrow with mining tools and portable water tank that the early prospectors pushed around the goldfields of Western Australia.

2   The cyclad palms of the Kimberley area of Western Australia. These palms date back to prehistoric times when Australia was part of the great southern super-continent, more than 160 million years ago.

See also plates 35 to 42.

3   One of the gigantic Euclid trucks at Hamersley mine at Tom Price, Western Australia. They carry about 300 tonnes.

4   Jack holding forth next to Paddy Hannan's statue in the centre or Kalgoorlie, Western Australia. Hannan discovered gold in this district in 1893.

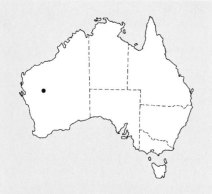

Situated in the mineral-rich Pilbara region, the Hamersley is Western Australia's highest mountain range. The red kangaroo lives in the dry inland plains of all mainland states. It is the world's largest marsupial, the mature male reaching up to two metres in height.

1 BIG RED

I've spent a lot of time around the magnificent Hamersley Range of Western Australia. It is an area that fascinates me, and I never seem to tire of going there. I return every year or so, and just take in the scenery. Then I paint it. On this particular trip it had been a good season, and there was plenty of wildlife around. Waterbirds could be seen on almost every bit of water, and big red kangaroos were in vast numbers. They would have moved into the area when the rains came. The plentiful wildlife made this a real pleasure to paint.

Coolyjarra is in South Australia's magnificent Everard Range.
The English-born explorer Ernest Giles is best known for crossing the Nullarbor Plain from Beltana, South Australia, to Perth in 1875-6. His route was much further north than that of Eyre, and he returned by a route that was even further north again. Giles died in Coolgardie in 1897, aged 62.

OPPOSITE PAGE:

Coolyjarra
Oil on canvas, 76 x 51 cm

2 COOLYJARRA

Coolyjarra was a very special place for the Aborigines of this area. The evidence suggests that they camped at the back of this rock for something like 18 000 years. On that side (the north side) was a well with water only a metre below the surface.

Ernest Giles, one of our early explorers, camped here on his travels across Australia. In fact, he had trouble with the Aborigines in this area simply because he camped right on the water. To make matters worse, the Aborigines had never seen camels before and would have been frightened of them.

One of my very dear friends here is Kuntjy. When I first went to this area he was the head man, the elder of the council. Kuntjy used to come away painting with me and explain all about the scenery, such as where the snake came from in the Dreamtime and the story of Coolyjarra. Kuntjy was about eighteen when he saw his first white man — and his first camels. He told me he was petrified with fear by those animals. Kuntjy is now more than 100 years old. He's a wonderful person.

If you follow the road around to the other side of Coolyjarra you'll come across Betty's Well, which can be seen in the following painting.

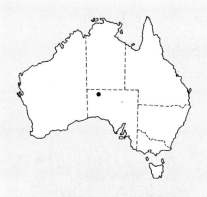

In recent years, state and federal governments have made an effort to compensate the Aboriginal people for the many injustices perpetrated against them over the past two centuries. Everard Park Station was restored to the Aboriginal people under the *Pitjantjatjara Land Rights Act* introduced in South Australia in 1981.

OPPOSITE PAGE:

Betty's Well
Oil on canvas, 68.5 x 46 cm

3 BETTY'S WELL

When the Europeans first came to settle in this country they needed water for their cattle and horses. The Aborigines, who had been living in this area for at least 18 000 years, were hunted off their well, and the new settlers put a windmill on it to pump the water into a tank for their stock. The water was very good, a plentiful supply, and only one metre below ground — a real treasure in this type of country. Today it's called Betty's Well.

Everard Park Station, as this property became known, was owned by a succession of white people for many years. However, it is now owned by the Aborigines who run some cattle on it. They call it Mimili which means 'the place before the white man came'. It has always been a very special place to the Aborigines, for this is the land of the Pitjantjatjara people. My friend Kuntjy told me that before the European settlers came his mother used to live in the gunyah [Aboriginal bush hut] by the tree.

Rawnsley Bluff is part of Wilpena Pound (the western rim), a vast natural amphitheatre ringed by sheer cliffs, situated in the Flinders Ranges. This stunning area is of special spiritual significance to the Aborigines; there are several ancient rock carvings and paintings at Arkaroo Rock on the slopes of Rawnsley Bluff, and at the nearby Sacred Canyon.

OPPOSITE PAGE:
Rawnsley Bluff
Oil on canvas, 68.5 x 46 cm

4 RAWNSLEY BLUFF

As you are travelling from Hawker, about 10 kilometres fom Wilpena, you'll see Rawnsley Bluff right in front of you. In the late afternoon it's a beautiful sight. There's a sign pointing to a turn-off to the left, five or six kilometres before you get to Wilpena. That road goes into the Rawnsley Bluff camping complex. As you enter you cross a gum creek — the spot I chose for this painting.

Rawnsley Bluff is a part of the western side of Wilpena Pound. Lots of people who know the ranges camp in this area rather than going right into the Pound. The reason for this is that every night as the sun sets Rawnsley Bluff looks different — but always spectacular. If you go further in you are too close and you seem to be hemmed in. To see these ranges at their best you need to be a kilometre or so back from them, in the early morning or late afternoon.

The spectacular Kimberley district in the far north of Western Australia is a vast Precambrian sandstone plateau of about 356000 square kilometres, bounded by the sea to the north and west. It is proving very rich in minerals, especially diamonds. Gold was discovered at Hall's Creek in 1883, and sheep and cattle have been grazed in the area since the end of the 19th century.

OPPOSITE PAGE:
Mable Downs Cattle Station
Oil on canvas, 68.5 x 46 cm

5 MABLE DOWNS CATTLE STATION

I never get tired of painting this area of the Kimberley. The scenery on this cattle station has to be seen to be believed. I painted this on the way from Turkey Creek on the turn-off to Texas Downs Station. This used to be the road into the Bungle Bungles. Now you have to go in by another road about 45 kilometres further south. This is a shocking road — the first time I went in that way it took five hours to do 50 kilometres.

Mable Downs is on the main road from Kununurra to Hall's Creek, about 30 kilometres south of Turkey Creek. I come here every year to paint the spectacular scenery. My wife Mary and I love it here. Harry and Lorna Rigg, who have managed the place for many years, always make us feel welcome.

Rabbits were first brought to Australia with the First Fleet in 1788. However, they did not become a problem until Thomas Austin imported wild rabbits for hunting on his property near Geelong, Victoria, in 1859. In less than ten years they were considered a disaster in Victoria's Western District. And by the early years of the 20th century they had reached all states, but they did not thrive in the far north.

OPPOSITE PAGE:
Underground Mutton
Oil on canvas, 61 x 41 cm

6 UNDERGROUND MUTTON

One day I pulled up at this scene at Mootooroo Station, 100 kilometres south-west of Broken Hill, and decided to paint it. There was only one rabbit out when I first arrived, but because I kept quiet they gradually started to pop out of their burrows as the day wore on. When they had decided there was no danger they started to go to the bushes at the edge of the burrows. This painting is simple yet I feel it works, and is a typically Australian scene — the kind of place you could come across in most parts of the country.

Over the years the rabbit has become a big problem for Australia, costing us millions of dollars a year. I have seen country completely devastated by them. I was coming down from Queensland a few years ago and when I got to where the dog-proof netting turns from the New South Wales/South Australian border to go direct west, the rabbits were piled up against the fence in the corner, up to two metres high. The last ones were hopping over the top of this 'living wall'. They were moving south, as they do every November.

The Pinnacles Desert is about 200 kilometres north of Perth. It was made part of Nambung National Park in 1968, and is popular with tourists in spring when the surrounding hills are carpeted with wildflowers.

OPPOSITE PAGE:
Pinnacles Desert
Oil on canvas, 91.5 x 61cm

7 PINNACLES DESERT

In Nambung National Park you'll see one of the most astonishing sights to be found anywhere in Australia — these extraordinary limestone pillars of different shapes and sizes. Drive about 200 kilometres north from Perth and you'll come to a little spot called Cervantes. A few kilometres inland and there they are.

You'd think a mad sculptor had been let loose on the place to do as he pleased. Some of these monoliths stand five metres in height and some are no bigger than your thumb. All the pillars have different names — there's the Garden Wall, the Camel, the Kangaroo and the Elephant's Foot, as well as the Milk Bottles, The Molars, the Three Sisters and Madonna. How these misshapen clusters of limestone got here has puzzled generations of experts. A combination of limestone, sand, shell deposits, wind and rain have formed them. Nobody can be quite sure how old they are but people reckon the Pinnacles have been around for something like 25 000–30 000 years.

This whole region is accessible by conventional vehicles for about 15 kilometres alongside the coast. If you are ever in this area, do yourself a favour and have a look at the 'abandoned city' that is the Pinnacles Desert.

Napier Range is in the south-western area of the Kimberley, and runs parallel with the road from Fitzroy Crossing to Derby for over 200 kilometres. Fitzroy Crossing is a tiny settlement, about 270 kilometres inland from Derby, where the road crosses the Fitzroy River.

8 NAPIER RANGE

This range could easily have been called 'The Barrier' because when you leave Fitzroy Crossing going west to Derby it runs parallel to the road for nearly the whole distance — a few hundred kilometres. The early settlers must have had quite a problem with it because they would have found it impossible to get their stock over. They would have had to travel until they could find an opening — and there aren't too many.

The windmill shown here is pumping water through a pipeline from one tank to another, some kilometres away. This particular scene is one I've come across many times — a leaking pipeline that provides a watering point for the animals.

OPPOSITE PAGE:

Napier Range
Oil on canvas, 76.5 x 51 cm

The Flinders Ranges extend in an unbroken chain for about 430 kilometres from Peterborough in the south to the harsh inland region near Lake Eyre. They are renowned for their spectacular scenery, wealth of wildlife and rich vegetation.

OPPOSITE PAGE:
Brachina Gorge
Oil on canvas, 61 x 40.5 cm

9 BRACHINA GORGE

I painted this scene on my last visit to the Flinders Ranges. I had often looked at Brachina Gorge but, because you are surrounded by it, it's difficult to get back far enough for a really good vantage point. You just can't seem to see over the mountains. But this time I found a good spot. While I was doing this painting a kangaroo and her joey came hopping across the road. She stopped to see where he was, and so I put them in the painting. I think they add a wonderful touch. I always try to include the things that are happening in the landscape. When you do this you capture a wonderful moment in time.

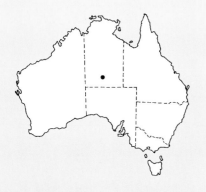

Albert Namatjira, a member of the Aranda tribe, was the first Aborigine to adopt the European style of painting. His watercolours of Central Australia soon attracted critical acclaim, bringing him fame and wealth. Tragically, however, Namatjira became caught between two worlds, and was gaoled for supplying his people with alcohol — an offence at the time. He died soon after being released from gaol in 1959.

OPPOSITE PAGE:

Mount Sonder
Oil on canvas, 91.5 x 61.5 cm

10 MOUNT SONDER

This was the homeland of Albert Namatjira and until he painted it the white population had not taken much notice of it. Since that time it has become famous and today it is one of the most visited tourist spots in Australia. Now there's a sealed road from Alice Springs right through to Mount Sonder and Glen Helen Gorge. This has made it much more accessible. Everybody visiting Alice Springs should drive out to this area, because this is one of the real treasure spots in Australia.

I've included two paintings of Mount Sonder in this book. You could paint it every day from a different position and every scene would be quite different. I have even considered doing a whole book of paintings of Mount Sonder. I think it would be fascinating if I could capture her in all her moods. Why do I say 'her'? It's because the Aborigines call this mountain the Sleeping Lubra.

Archaeologists believe that Aborigines have been living in this northern area of Australia for at least 50 000 years. The ancestors of the Aborigines are thought to have arrived from Asia via island bridges and canoes. Arnhem Land is the largest Aboriginal reserve in Australia, covering about 97 000 square kilometres. It includes Kakadu National Park, which contains the oldest Aboriginal camping site to have been dated.

OPPOSITE PAGE:

The Get-together
Oil on canvas, 40.5 x 30.5 cm
Private collection

11 THE GET-TOGETHER

I have been painting nocturne scenes from the start of my painting career, and have found they have a special appeal for many people. At one of my first art shows Sir Eric Lanker, who opened the exhibition, said that if a particular nocturne painting of mine had not been sold he would have advised the Australian National Gallery to buy it.

This particular scene is of a group of Aborigines at a get-together on the Roper River in Arnhem Land. You often used to see them around their fires. I decided to paint these Aborigines in white man's dress, with the light showing on their shirts and dresses. It's a change for me as I usually depict them in their traditional clothing.

At the junction of the Strzelecki and Cooper creeks, Innamincka Station is one of the largest cattle stations in the country. Explorers Burke and Wills died within 10 kilometres of the present homestead. Charles Sturt was in the area in 1845, giving his name to Sturt's Stony Desert.

OPPOSITE PAGE:

The Stone-age Craftsman
Oil on canvas, 40.5 x 30.5 cm
Private collection

12 THE STONE-AGE CRAFTSMAN

For more than seven years, my Uncle Ron was the manager of Innamincka Station which was (and is still) owned by the Kidman family. Ron knew that I was interested in Aboriginal artefacts — in how they were made and what they were used for. On this particular trip he took me into Sturt's Stony Desert. As the name suggests, there are stones as far as the eye can see. He showed me this spot where for thousands of years the Aborigines had chipped stones to form them into tools. Over the ages, the chippings had built up to a mound of about one-and-a-half metres. That scene is what I've tried to depict here.

The Bungle Bungle Ranges consist of ancient sandstone domes and spires which rise to 450 metres above the grassland plains. This remote, unspoilt area is at the centre of many Aboriginal myths, and is one of the most extraordinary landscapes in Australia. The Bungle Bungles cover an area in excess of 700 square kilometres.

OPPOSITE PAGE:

Texas Downs Station
Oil on canvas, 68.5 x 45.5 cm

13 TEXAS DOWNS STATION

Texas Downs is in the Kimberley region in Western Australia. I always pass through it on my way to the Bungle Bungles. There's a road that turns off the main highway, just past Turkey Creek, that goes out to the homestead.

I think the boab trees give a nice touch to these landscapes and I find it interesting that you often see three young trees clumped together. Of course when I see a beautiful scene like this I just have to paint it. This wonderful area is well worth a visit for anybody going this way.

Archaeological evidence proves that Australian Aborigines have been fashioning boomerangs for at least 8000 years. Fragments of she-oak boomerangs were found in a peat bog near Millicent on South Australia's south-east coast, in 1975. They were carbon-dated as being between 8000 and 10 000 years old.

14 THE BOOMERANG-MAKER

On some of my first painting trips I went into the Everard Range. I would get Kuntjy, who was one of the elders of the council of the Pitjantjatjara people, to come away painting with me. I mentioned to him that I would like to see an Aborigine making a boomerang. So Kuntjy arranged for some of his tribesmen to do this while I painted the scene. I had often seen Aborigines making boomerangs when I was a child, but it didn't mean anything to me then. But to see them do it now was really something very special.

Sir Sidney Kidman, known as the 'Cattle King', owned two huge chains of cattle stations, one stretching from the Channel Country through to western New South Wales, and the other through Central Australia to northern South Australia. At the peak of his success, Kidman owned more land than any single person in the British Empire. This classic woolshed is a familiar landmark in the Andamooka area.

15 ARCOONA SHEARING SHED

This is probably one of the best-known of Kidman's shearing sheds. It is within 100 metres of the main road to the Andamooka opal fields, so thousands of people see it every year. Many years ago my Uncle Andy used to work the Andamooka opal fields. Every time he went broke he would move on to Arcoona Station. There he would get a job as a stockman, and his wife Joyce would be the cook. They would stop there until they had built up a bank and then they would go back to the opal fields. Throughout those years, from 1940 to 1965, I spent a lot of time calling into Arcoona and going out with the manager Nick Moody. He would take me out to look at all the Aboriginal campsites which are quite prolific through this area.

Mick was a wonderful amateur anthropologist. He donated something like 27 000 Aboriginal perie points [pointed stone tools] to the Adelaide Museum over the years. You find most of them where there's water, but unfortunately with the cattle coming in to drink, they get broken up and ruined. So rather than see this happen Mick collected the artefacts and put them in museums for future generations to see.

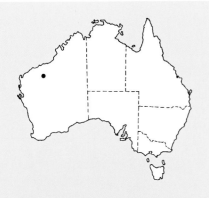

Over millions of years, the Fortescue and Ashburton rivers have gashed deep gorges into the ancient rock strata of the Hamersley Range. The lush green vegetation around the gorges provides a dramatic contrast to the dry brown plains of the plateau surface.

16 DALE'S GORGE, HAMERSLEY RANGE

The Hamersley Range is one of the most rugged but beautiful places in Western Australia. To see Dale's Gorge in the late afternoon light is quite spectacular and very special. It's a wonderful area. I could spend six months wandering around in there and not get tired of it; there is always something different to see. It's even better if you have someone who knows the area to show you around. I have been fortunate in having some good friends from Perth, Ralph and Penny Smith, who first took Mary and me into the Hamersley Range. Then a couple of years later a ranger showed me around. Later still, when I made a film there, I had a lot of help from the National Parks and station people in the area.

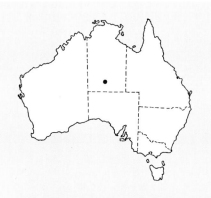

Aboriginal artist Abert Namatjira was probably the first person to bring the vivid purples, blues and reds of Central Australia to public consciousness. This magnificent ancient mountain, famous for its changes of mood according to the time of day, is situated 80 kilometres west of Alice Springs.

OPPOSITE PAGE:
The Sleeping Lubra
Oil on canvas, 114 x 76 cm

17 THE SLEEPING LUBRA — MOUNT SONDER

This mountain has fascinated me from the first time I saw it. I come to this area every time I go north, and I nearly always paint it. Each time I choose a different spot and a different time of day. This is the land of the Aranda people, Namatjira's homeland. When you look at country like this you begin to understand why the Aborigines love their land and why it means so much to them.

You can easily see why the Aborigines call Mount Sonder the Sleeping Lubra. She is very well endowed. When you look at the Finke River just below it you couldn't imagine that little creek causing problems. But the railway line had to be re-routed from up north (Quorn, Marree, Oodnadatta way) to west from Port Augusta to Tarcoola, then up to Alice Springs. Every time they got a good rain the line was washed away. The culprit was the Finke River.

The picturesque Flinders Ranges are home to a wealth of bird, reptile and animal life, including the rare yellow-footed rock wallaby. There are several national parks in this area, the largest of which is the Flinders Ranges National Park (about 78 500 hectares).

18 FLINDERS RANGES

Every time I visit the Flinders Ranges I look for something different, so I can show them from a new angle or perspective. To get this view I had to climb up to a high position and on a greater angle than I usually choose. This painting came together right from the start. I am very pleased with it because I feel I have captured the beauty and mood of this area. I got a lot of pleasure out of painting this magnificent scene.

OPPOSITE PAGE:

Flinders Ranges
Oil on canvas, 76 x 51 cm
Private collection

Living conditions are still extremely harsh in the remote opal-mining town of Andamooka. It gets so hot that most residents live in semi-undergound dugouts, built from local materials. These rough dwellings are usually covered with white material called copi, which consists of millions of microscopic seashells.

19 CAMP FOR THE NIGHT — NOCTURNE

The first time I saw a scene like this I was a boy of ten. I had two uncles who were at the Andamooka opal fields and I used to love going there to see them. The Aborigines were still in their tribes then and you would often see a tribe of about 150 come along and camp by a type of oasis which we called a donga. *They would stay there while the food lasted and was reasonably easy to get. Then one morning you would get up and they would be gone. They had moved on to another campsite.*

I painted this scene north of Andamooka opal fields, in the area known as North Well. I have shown how it used to look, with all the campfires in the moonlight, and shadowy figures moving around. I have painted night scenes for nearly twenty years, and you learn something every time you do one. They gradually become better and better. I feel that I am at last able to capture the mood of the night, as I've always wanted to. The night has always been special to me.

Boabs grow only in the far north of Australia. Sometimes called bottle trees because of the swollen shape of their trunks, they are only in leaf during the Wet Season. This is also the time when their exotic, tubular creamy flowers appear.

OPPOSITE PAGE:

The Land of the Boabs
Oil on canvas, 68.5 x 46 cm

20 THE LAND OF THE BOABS

I painted this while staying at Mable Downs Station which is about 30 kilometres south of Turkey Creek, on the main road to Hall's Creek. This area is one of the most magnificent parts of Australia. Mable Downs country runs to the very edge of the Bungle Bungles. In fact you drive on Mable Downs country when you go into the Bungles. I love this region. I spend three or four weeks here every year and, after eight years, I believe I am just starting to understand it and to get a feel for it.

The boabs have a special fascination for me. You will often see a big tree with all the young trees around it, as if it's a mother with her family around her. In a way I suppose that is really what it is. Then with a few ant-hills tangled up amongst them you have the makings of an interesting painting. You only come across a scene like this in a couple of areas in Australia, so that makes it rather special.

Birds and animals miraculously appear after the flooding of the Channel Country of inland Queensland and north-east South Australia, following the northern monsoons. The overflow of the Georgina, Hamilton and Diamantina rivers and Cooper Creek forms hundreds of channels in this usually-arid area. Later, the water sinks into the earth and the area becomes arid once more.

OPPOSITE PAGE:

Waterbirds
Oil on canvas, 68.5 x 46 cm

21 WATERBIRDS

When the big cyclones sweep in from the Gulf of Carpentaria all these waterways in the northern part of Australia flood. To see the Channel Country of the Cooper Creek in flood is really something. In parts it flows out to a width of 200 kilometres.

The largest chain of cattle stations in the British Empire was centred on this great Channel Country of the northern part of Australia. It was founded by Sir Sidney Kidman at the end of the last century.

A typical droving team consisted of three men (and a cook) to about every 3000 head of cattle. They travelled enormous distances through the arid inland plains. The Birdsville Track from Queensland to South Australia was one of the most famous cattle routes.

22 THE LAST BIG MOB

Years ago when I worked in the bush you would see scenes like this quite often, as the drovers brought the mobs of Kidman cattle down along the border fence and onto the southern markets. In this painting I have tried to capture one of my best mates with a very big mob, 5000 head of cattle. He would bring them down to Forter's Station near Cockburn, on the New South Wales/South Australian border. There they would be divided up. Some would be put on on the train to go to Adelaide markets, others sold to Broken Hill butchers, and so on.

My mate's name was Jack Dickson. He drove Kidman's cattle for many years and had no peer as a drover and stockman. He often said to me that it doesn't matter how big the mob is as long as you've got a good leader. This was usually a bull or bullock that would get out in front and keep walking, then all the rest would follow. When I look at this painting I feel I've succeeded in capturing this scene from the past.

Cooper Creek is formed by the junction of the Thomson and Barcoo rivers, and it flows through Queensland and north-east South Australia towards Lake Eyre. Discovered by Charles Sturt in 1845, it is the lifeblood of the surrounding cattle country.

OPPOSITE PAGE:
Cooper Creek
Oil on canvas, 91.5 x 61 cm

23 COOPER CREEK

I've painted scenes like this many times. Every time I go to Cooper Creek I do some more, and I always seem to be able to find a new spot to paint. I must admit I have a soft spot for the birdlife of this area. Because water is scarce here the ordinary birds of the bush are always plentiful, as well as the waterbirds, which are in their thousands.

Once, when I was making a film in the area, I had told the director that when we arrived there would be thousands of birds. But when we got to Lake Coongi there were in fact very few birds around. The director looked at me and asked me where they were. I just told him to set the camera up. When he was ready I fired a shot. Instantly there were thousands of birds flying about — a most remarkable sight.

Mount Tom Price to the west of the Hamersley Range National Park and Mount Newman, to the south-east, provide Australia with most of its iron-ore reserves. In fact, these ranges are probably the site of the richest and largest deposits of iron ore in the world. The Hamersley is the highest mountain range in Western Australia, the highest point of which is Mount Meharry (1250 metres).

OPPOSITE PAGE:
The Hamersleys
Oil on canvas, 68.5 x 46 cm

24 THE HAMERSLEYS

I love to paint these spectacular rock faces, especially if there is a waterhole or creek down below. When this is the case you get this wonderful birdlife and animals coming in to water. You often see seagulls at these spots, sometimes up to 500 kilometres from the sea.

The city of Broken Hill, the site of the world's richest lead-silver-zinc ore deposits, is a man-made oasis in the arid district of far western New South Wales. It was first mined in the 1870s, but known deposits are now running out. The North Mine was closed in 1993.

OPPOSITE PAGE:

North Mine
Oil on canvas, 114 x 76 cm

25 NORTH MINE

I never feel like painting mining scenes, or buildings for that matter. But when the closing of the North Mine was announced I decided that I should make an exception, because it would soon be dismantled. I suppose this was my way of preserving a part of Broken Hill's history. When I had finished the painting, and had it framed, I was very pleased with it. I felt that I had captured the feeling of the mine and a bit of the mystique that went with it.

The cliffs surrounding Wilpena
Pound are famous for their
spectacular changes of colour at
different times of day. Wilpena
Pound dates back to the
Cambrian era, and is of great
significance to the Aboriginal
people. They have inhabited
this area for over 30 000 years.

26 THE WILPENAS

Probably the most spectacular area in the Flinders Ranges is around Wilpena Pound. There are few places in Australia that can rival this particular spot. I did this painting a few years ago as a present for my wife Mary. I was very pleased with it and Mary loved it, so nothing else matters. I think it's wonderful that artists have the ability to produce a special work to suit a special person. It's most gratifying. All artists put a bit of themselves into such paintings.

The German-born artist Sir Hans Heysen arrived in Australia, aged 16, in 1884. He is best-known for his paintings of massive gum trees, and mostly painted around South Australia's Flinders and Mount Lofty ranges. He received the Wynne Prize for landscape painting nine times.

27 MOUNT ALEX

I did this painting on the same trip that I painted the Wilpenas (the previous painting).
My wife Mary liked them both, so she finished up with them. Now they hang on the same wall — they look good together.
I often wonder what Hans Heysen thought when he first saw the Flinders Ranges. I believe he was one of the first artists to paint them, and that he had a special caravan made so that he could camp out in selected areas.

OPPOSITE PAGE:

Mount Alex
Oil on canvas, 46 x 30.5 cm
Artist's family collection

The East Kimberley region is famous for its breathtaking scenery of majestic mountains and lush, irrigated fields. The town of Kununurra, 3200 kilometres north-east of Perth, is the service centre for the surrounding area.

28 THE ROCK FACE

As you drive from Kununurra to Hall's Creek the scenery is probably unequalled anywhere in Australia. Early morning or late afternoon is magic. The light at those times is what I've tried to capture in this painting. These rock faces have always been special to me, and every time I see them the colour is different from last time. They change all day as the sun's rays alter the angles.

You leave Kununurra with the spectacular Carr Boyd Range, then as you turn off the Wyndham Road you have the Cockburn Range on your right. As you go south, you'll see range after range, every one of them having something different about it. At one spot you go through an area just like the Devil's Marbles, then you come to hundreds of big gum creeks and boabs by the thousands. I painted this scene about 100 kilometres south of Kununurra.

Glen Helen Gorge, in the Macdonnell Ranges, was carved out over millions of years by the Finke River. There are many waterholes surrounded by lush vegetation within the gorge. Spectacular rock formations include the Giant's Staircase and the Vertical Rocks.

OPPOSITE PAGE:
Glen Helen Gorge
Oil on canvas, 114 x 76 cm

29 GLEN HELEN GORGE

When I was painting The Sleeping Lubra *(plate 17) I decided to paint Glen Helen Gorge as well. I simply turned my back on the Sleeping Lubra and I was looking straight at Glen Helen Gorge. I blocked it in on the canvas and waited for the right light to finish it.*

I have always found a certain peace while watching the Finke River flow past me. It eventually finishes up in Lake Eyre. The Finke River has caused the railways a lot of trouble over the years. It's amazing when you think of it. It's not a spectacularly large river, like the Murray, but when it gets in flood it really causes a lot of damage — sometimes over its entire length of some 3000 kilometres.

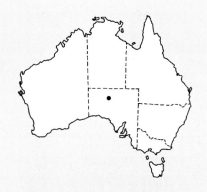

This magnificent country is the land of the Pitjantjatjara people. Archaeological evidence indicates that Aborigines have been living in this area for at least 18 000 years.

30 ABORIGINAL STOCKMEN

For me, one of the most special places in Australia is the Everard Range. All this area, halfway between Coober Pedy and Alice Springs, is mostly Aboriginal lands. To be in the Everards in the late afternoon light is an unbelievable experience, and to see a scene like this is a real bonus. The stockmen shifting a mob of cattle to better feed adds to the interest of the painting.

OPPOSITE PAGE:
Aboriginal Stockmen
Oil on canvas, 113 x 76 cm

With their natural horsemanship and affinity with the land, Aboriginal stockmen were the mainstay of the outback cattle stations in the last century and early this century, thriving in climatic conditions which most European-born settlers found unendurable.

31 SHIFTING THE MOB

When I've been in the Everard Range I've often seen Aborigines working the cattle. Go to most of the cattle stations throughout Australia today, especially in Queensland, the Northern Territory and the north of South Australia, and you'll still see Aboriginal stockmen. They seem to have a special affinity with cattle; they handle them very well. They also seem to really enjoy the work — you'll see them laughing and joking as they work. And they go to all the rodeos they can get to as well. This particular scene was painted when I was making a film for the ABC. I believe that if it was not for the Aboriginal stockmen, Australia wouldn't be at its present stage of development, because for many years they were the main workers of the cattle industry.

The story of Silverton is typical of mining towns all over Australia. Silver was discovered in 1883, attracting thousands of people to this desolate area. However, the field mine was closed six years later and most settlers headed for what is now Broken Hill, leaving Silverton a virtual ghost town.

OPPOSITE PAGE:
Churches of Silverton
Oil on canvas, 76 x 51 cm
Private collection

32 CHURCHES OF SILVERTON

Many films have been made at Silverton, an old mining town 26 kilometres from Broken Hill. I think this is because of its real Australian atmosphere and landscape. Over the years I have driven past this spot about two hundred times coming and going from the bush. One day, when I first started painting, I decided to paint these churches. They used to cater for more than 5000 people when Silverton was in its prime. Today they have been converted into art galleries by several local artists, and are popular tourist attractions. Considering their age and the harsh weather conditions they have endured, they are in reasonable shape.

I have included this painting just to show how I used to look at things when I first started painting about twenty years ago. My daughter, Christine, loved it so I gave it to her.

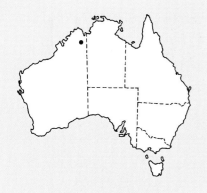

Lake Argyle, Australia's largest freshwater lake, was artificially created in 1970-72 as the second stage of the Ord River irrigation scheme. The Ord River rises in the East Kimberley and flows north to Cambridge Gulf.

OPPOSITE PAGE:

A Bend in the Ord River
 Oil on canvas, 46 x 30.5 cm

33 A BEND IN THE ORD RIVER

On my travels this year I pulled up at the fruit-fly roadblock on the border of the Northern Territory and Western Australia. The chaps there told me that the boss ranger wanted to see me. I contacted him in Kununurra and he said that he would like to show me a spot on the Ord River where it flows toward Wyndham, then into the sea. He wanted me to paint it for him.

He called around on Saturday morning at 8 am. My wife Mary and I got into his Landrover and for the next ten hours the scenery was magic. It was worth being thrown around on a dirt road for half a day. We followed the Ord River overland to the sea. After it flows into Lake Argyle it then continues on into Cambridge Gulf, into which most of Western Australia's fresh water flows. This is a terrible waste; it should be piped down to Perth.

This part of the Ord River is the ranger's special spot where he often goes fishing, hoping to catch a barramundi. The brilliant light and clarity of the air and scenery was what attracted me most of all. The whole area is completely pollution-free and has the effect of looking as if it has all just been washed.

Mulyungarie Station runs north from Cockburn along the South Australia/New South Wales border for 150 kilometres. As you travel north it is the last sheep station in the area — beyond it there are only cattle stations. Dingoes were trapped and killed because of the damage they caused to livestock. Australia's first introduced animal, the dingo is believed to have been brought to Australia by a comparatively late migration of Aborigines, about 4000 years ago.

OPPOSITE PAGE:
The Dogger and his Dog
Oil on canvas, 76 x 51 cm
Artist's family collection

34 THE DOGGER AND HIS DOG

When I first went onto Mulyungarie Station in South Australia, thirty years ago, they used to employ a dogger. His job was to get rid of the dingoes on the property. The dogger at this time was a chap by the name of Jack Dickson who had spent most of his life as a drover for Kidman. He was the one who told me to always carry a pack of playing cards when travelling in the bush. I put this hint into my book Safe Outback Travel.

Jack was always out and about checking his traps or looking for dog tracks to tell him where the dingoes were camping. He was a familiar sight. When I showed him this painting, he looked at it for about fifteen minutes, then tears started to roll down his cheeks.

I painted this scene in 1973, six months after I first took up painting. When I tried to sell it for $50, at that time, nobody wanted to buy it. So my family still owns it and now I'm glad that nobody bought it.

PAINTINGS DONE FOR TELEVISION PROGRAMS

I have included this section because so many people have asked me what happened to a certain painting they saw me do on television. Sometimes it was hard to know how to start a program off or how to depict a certain event, so I'd do a painting to help me out. The main trouble was that I was never given enough time to finish them.

Bob Plasto, one of the directors I worked with, would say, 'You can have as much time as you like'. So I'd get all my gear out, get organized and start painting. After, say, ten minutes, he would come over and ask how it was going. 'Fair go,' I'd say, 'I've just started.' Then he would look at the effort and say 'That's looking good. I think we'll go with that.' So I think the longest I ever had to work on a painting was thirty minutes. This certainly taught me to get on with it and not sit around when Plasto was in charge.

Photographs

THIS PAGE:

- This is a *namma* hole, a rockhole which fills with water that runs off the rocks, in Coolgardie, Western Australia.
- A typical scene when filming in the outback.
- The prison tree at Coolgardie, Western Australia. There were once about twenty of these 'prisons'. They were mainly used to protect intoxicated people from falling down mine shafts, until they had sobered up.

OPPOSITE PAGE:

- Karle's Crossing on the East Alligator River.

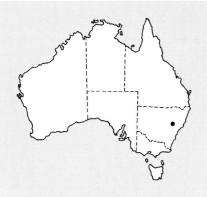

Young is in the western foothills of the Great Dividing Range. Now the centre of a fruit-growing area, it was once a gold-mining town, and the scene of the infamous Lambing Flat riots of 1861, in which Australian and European miners forcibly demonstrated their resentment of Chinese miners.

OPPOSITE PAGE:

Ready to Harvest
Oil on canvas, 68.5 x 46 cm
Private collection

35 READY TO HARVEST

I was asked to go over to Young, in New South Wales, to do a painting of a wheatfield to be used in a commercial. I warned the producer that I had never painted wheat before, largely because there isn't much wheat in the areas I go to. It was a nice scene. The wheat was alive which I was determined to capture. I was very pleased with the end result. Young is a pleasant place, and is especially known for its wonderful cherries. I have always dodged painting rural scenes but when I look at this one and also the one of sugar cane (plate 36), I think that maybe I should widen my horizons.

Sugar is one of Australia's most valuable crops; we are one of the world's leading sugar producers. Sugar is grown along the Queensland coast and in northern New South Wales.

OPPOSITE PAGE:

Japoon Valley
Oil on canvas, 68.5 x 46 cm
Private collection

36 JAPOON VALLEY

Like the previous painting, this was done for a commercial. This time it was on sugar cane, in Northern Queensland. Here again, I had never painted sugar cane before, and mused that it would be an experience for all of us. There was something very special about the scene. I walked around looking at it for about thirty minutes before I started. I was a little apprehensive at the beginning because of my lack of knowledge on the subject, but I was very pleased with the result. I believe you paint best the country you know best. But I also believe that every so often a move to something different is important for your development as an artist.

The farmer who owned the property watched me do this painting. Then he wanted to buy the finished product. I was flattered but the company who had commissioned it had the first option. As it turned out this company did buy it, and then gave it away as a prize in a competition.

The last of the full-blooded Tasmanian Aborigines is believed to have been Truganini, the daughter of the chief of Bruny Island. She died in 1876 at the age of 73. The rest of her people had either been slaughtered by English settlers or had died from their diseases, to which they had little resistance.

OPPOSITE PAGE:

Captain Cook's Landing on Bruny Island
Oil on canvas, 61 x 40.5 cm

37 CAPTAIN COOK'S LANDING ON BRUNY ISLAND

In this painting I've tried to capture exactly what happened on this day. The ship would have been at sea for about three months. They wouldn't have known exactly where they were when they suddenly came upon a safe harbour, Adventure Bay. They dropped anchor and went ashore at Bruny Island, where they would have found fresh water, probably fresh meat as well, and even fresh fruits. It must have been the first time in months that they had stepped onto solid ground. It would have been a joyous occasion.

The reason I have painted Aborigines on the beach is to show that this day was also a sad day. Today was going to be the start of the complete annihilation of a race of people. In less that 100 years there would not be a single Tasmanian Aborigine left.

I painted this for a television program on Tasmania. When I have a special painting I like to give it to special people. I gave this one to some very good friends for Christmas. They love it, so I'm happy.

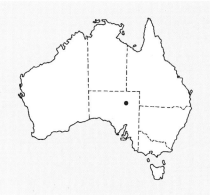

The Birdsville Track, which crosses Sturt's Stony Desert, is about 500 kilometres long, stretching from Marree, South Australia, to Birdsville, the most isolated settlement in Queensland. It is synonymous with the legendary courage of the early stockmen who drove their cattle from Queensland's Channel Country to the Adelaide market. In recent years the track has been improved, but most stock is now transported by road train.

38 Tom Kruse

Probably one of our best-known outback characters is Tom Kruse. For many years he was the mailman on the Birdsville Track when it was just that — a track. That was when you got bogged every time you tried to get over a sandhill. Tom has become a legend in his lifetime. I did this painting for the film, The Birdsville Track, *and I've tried to show what Tom had to put up with in those days. For example, it would have taken an average of three days to travel from Marree to Birdsville. Today it takes just five or six hours.*

Tom used to carry two lengths of water troughing in his vehicle. They weighed more than 50 kilograms each. When he got bogged he would get them out and put them in front of the wheels. He would then drive until they bogged again and kept repeating this procedure until he got over the sandhill. When he got out of the bog he would then have to carry the troughing down the sandhill and put it on the truck until the next time.

After seeing me doing this painting on television many people rang me trying to buy it. But Tom Kruse was always a very special friend of mine, and I believed that the painting should go to him. It was one of my greatest pleasures to present it to him.

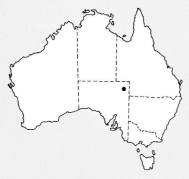

Captain Charles Sturt suffered great hardships in a series of expeditions between 1828 and 1846. In 1844 he set out from Adelaide in the hope of finding land in Central Australia. He followed the Murray and Darling rivers and then struck out north-west towards the Barrier Range near what is now Broken Hill. It was on this trip he discovered Sturt's Stony Desert and traced the Cooper Creek.

OPPOSITE PAGE:

Sturt Making Friends
Oil on canvas, 68.5 x 46 cm

39 STURT MAKING FRIENDS

Charles Sturt was a very good explorer. I have always attributed a great part of his success to his willingness to go out of his way to make friends with the Aborigines. I think he only had trouble with them on one occasion and that was at Fort Grey where they were camped at the time. Fort Grey is a freshwater lake near Cameron Corner, where the borders of South Australia, New South Wales and Queensland meet.

In this painting I tried to show what I believe would have happened many times — Sturt approaching the Aborigines and offering them bread, damper or meat. He always did this and in return they helped him with such things as finding waterholes. This was painted while I was making the film Steps of Charles Sturt. *In this I journey from Broken Hill to Cooper Creek, showing places Sturt visited on the way. The explorers Burke and Wills perished at roughly this spot on the Cooper.*

Many sailing ships foundered off the shores of this Bass Strait island in the last century. Today King Island is well-known for its high-class cheeses and other dairy products. It remains a picturesque island with beautiful sandy beaches on the north and east coasts, and rugged cliffs to the south.

OPPOSITE PAGE:

The Netherby
Oil on canvas, 61 x 40.5 cm

40 THE NETHERBY

This painting was done on location while I was making another film, King Island. *In my opinion this island should be named Magic Island — it's so beautiful.*

In 1866, a ship called the Netherby, *carrying 500 passengers and crew, was heading for Melbourne. During a storm at night it ran onto a reef about 500 metres from the island. This would have been a terrifying experience. Amazingly not one life was lost.*

There are many stories of survivors, but to me the most amazing one was of a woman and her two daughters. This woman decided that she and her daughters would have a better chance of survival if they made for the shore in the dark, instead of waiting for daylight. So, with a woollen rug, she got herself and her daughters over the side of the ship and then managed to swim to shore. To top off this incredible feat, she gave birth to a baby the next day.

In this painting I have shown what I thought the scene would have looked like, with the mother and daughters looking out to sea. The red rug covering the girls was later sent back to England, where it was kept in a museum for more than a hundred years. Only recently has it been returned to King Island, where it is now on display in a museum.

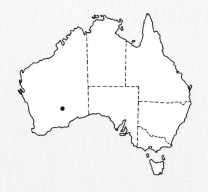

An Irishman, Paddy Hannan, discovered gold in the Kalgoorlie district in 1893, and the rush was on. By the turn of the century about 30 000 people had flocked to the area. The twin towns of Kalgoorlie and Boulder are centred on the famous 'Golden Mile' from which nearly 1000 tonnes of gold have been mined. Kanowna is just outside Kalgoorlie and was a booming town in its heyday. This area is still mined today.

OPPOSITE PAGE:

The Graveyard
Oil on canvas, 46 x 30.5 cm

41 THE GRAVEYARD

I came across this scene when I made Rainbow's End, *a film about the goldfields around Kalgoorlie. When we went out to a place called Kanowna there was a graveyard with diggings all over it. The warden explained that at the height of the gold rush it was found that the best run of gold was going into the graveyard. This of course was fenced off and no mining was allowed. A fellow called Murphy was elected to ask the warden for permission to mine beside the graves.*

The front headstone belonged to a chap named Wilson. So Murphy approached the warden and told him that he and Wilson used to be very good mates, and that he was sure Wilson wouldn't have minded them digging a little gold alongside him. So eventually the warden relented and they mined the cemetery. They took an amazing amount of gold out. I forget how much exactly, but it was something like 30 000 ounces (849 000 grams), all alluvial. It was taken from very shallow digging, and I don't suppose any of the cemetery residents objected. It is predictable that whenever you have stories of gold mines you always have a Murphy. They must have been an amazing family.

This painting is a reminder of the fragility of Australia's link with Europe during the days of sail. After many months at sea ships were often wrecked within sight of Australian shores. The arrival of a sailing ship was always an occasion for rejoicing — bringing as it did precious supplies, small luxuries and — best of all — news from the 'old country'.

OPPOSITE PAGE:

The Eye of the Wind
Oil on canvas, 114 x 76 cm

42 THE EYE OF THE WIND

When I was in Tasmania making the film Tasmania's Wild West *we used this ship, the* Eye of the Wind, *for the opening sequence and also to sail around parts of the west coast. This wonderful vessel takes tourist trips all over the world. The more I saw the ship the more fascinated I became with it, so I decided that I should try and paint it. This was my first painting of a ship at sea, and so I was very interested to see how much trouble I would get into. But it all came together straight away, and I was very pleased with the result.*

The producer/director, John Mabey, decided to use this painting in the film. As it finishes they roll the credits over it. I think it is a nice painting to finish this book on.

I hope that reading this book gave you as much pleasure as I got from doing the paintings. Best wishes.

Jack Absalom

Pitinjarra Pty. Limited.
638 Chapple Street,
Broken Hill NSW 2880

First published 1996

Copyright © 1996 Pitinjarra Pty. Ltd.

Editor: Christine Bartley
Colour Separations: First Media Pty. Ltd.
Printed and Bound at: Griffin Colour

National Library of Australia
Cataloguing-in-Publication Data.

Absalom, Jack, 1927-.
  Absalom.

  ISBN 0 646 28427 4.

  1. Absalom, Jack, 1927- . I. Title.

759.994